SHELLY CAT BY THE SEA

Adventures at the Beach

Written & Illustrated by

Nancy Lee Artist By-the-Sea

Library of Congress Cataloging-in-Publication Data

Lee, Nancy

Shelly Cat By the Sea: Adventures at the Beach

ISBN – 978-0-9982071-1-7

1. Lee, Nancy   2. Nature   3. Coastal Regions and Shorelines

www.nldesignsbythesea.com

nancyleeartbythesea@gmail.com

The beauty of the sea, coastal wild life and the beach inspire me in so many ways. My art and nature photography reflect my love of the sea. "**Shelly Cat By the Sea: Adventures at the Beach**" is a book that will give you a glimpse of coastal nature on Southern California beaches. Come along with Shelly Cat and her two "marvelous" mice friends, Marv & Louis, as they go on lots of adventures at the beach. Experience the magic and beauty of the Pacific Ocean coastal environment where sea lions and harbor seals live, dolphins surf the waves, pelicans fly and dive for fish and sea gulls raise their polka-dotted chicks. Walk on the beach where hermit crabs live in tide pools, seaweeds wash up & sea shells scatter across the sand. Visit a marsh at the bay, gather pine nuts from pine trees and go grunion hunting by moon light.

"Shelly Cat By the Sea: Adventures at the Beach" will be enjoyed by both children and adults. The watercolor illustrations in this book are inspired by my life by the sea. I hope that this book will inspire others to love the sea and coast as much as I do. Enjoy your own grand adventure at the beach with Shelly Cat By the Sea, Marv & Louis!

Nancy Lee Artist By-the-Sea
"I carry this beauty in my heart." ™

Shelly Cat By the Sea is a pretty little white cat with a short tail who smiles all the time, even when she is sleeping. She loves to wear necklaces with sea shells and hearts. She likes to wear straw hats, too.

"I'm so glad that you are coming along with me to have adventures at the beach!" said Shelly Cat By the Sea.

Marv & Louis are Shelly Cat's best friends. Marv & Louis are two "marvelous" mice!

Marv is a mouse who likes to read and learn about new things and his favorite sea shell is the scallop shell. Marv is very protective of Louis and watches over him.

Louis is a bit younger than Marv and can be shy sometimes. Louis is a funny mouse who likes to carry a paper umbrella with him. He started carrying a paper drink umbrella after finding a package of them at the beach.

Marv & Louis are always excited to have adventures at the beach with Shelly Cat.

Shelly Cat woke up and said to Marv & Louis, "Let's go to the beach!"

"Yay!" said Marv & Louis and off they went to the beach.

It seemed to be a wonderful day to build a sand castle. Shelly cat pushed the sand together with her paws to make the castle. Marv smoothed down the sand. Look closely and you can see Marv's hand prints on the castle walls! Louis collected pretty Scallop sea shells from the beach to decorate the castle. What great teamwork! After the castle was finished, they all stepped back and admired their work.

Shelly Cat said, "Wouldn't it be wonderful if we really had a castle on the beach to live in?"

Marv & Louis said, "Yes, it would!"

One day while the three friends walked on the beach, it started pouring rain. Shelly Cat By the Sea immediately grabbed a large palm tree leaf and held it over her head so she wouldn't get wet.

"Quick," said Shelly Cat, "come stand under this palm leaf with me."

Marv came running up holding a Scallop sea shell over his head to keep him dry until he reached the palm leaf. Louis strolled up to Shelly Cat & Marv at a leisurely pace.

Louis told them, "Good thing that I have my umbrella to keep me dry."

Shelly Cat and Marv both smiled. Louis is such a funny mouse to think that a paper drink umbrella would keep him dry!

"It looks like there are a million sand dollars on the beach today!" said Shelly Cat.

Shelly Cat and Louis started collecting a big pile of sand dollars.

"If we take all these shells home and so does everyone else, will all the shells be gone from the beach?" asked Marv.

Shelly Cat said, "You know Marv, I think you're right. We should enjoy the shells at the beach, but not take them home."

Louis said, "Let's make a heart shape with the sand dollars!"

Shelly Cat and the mice had lots of fun arranging the sand dollars into a heart shape on the sand.

"Since we're leaving the shells at the beach, won't it be a nice surprise for someone to come along and find our sand dollar heart?" said Shelly Cat.

On the walk home, they happily thought about someone finding their sand dollar heart!

"What are these things all over the beach today?" asked Louis.

"Louis", Marv said, "they are kelp pods from seaweed growing in the ocean."

"Watch", Shelly Cat said as she pounced on a kelp pod and it made a popping sound.

Marv & Louis jumped back in surprise.

"Wow!" the two mice said together.

The mice weren't big enough to squash and pop the kelp pods. Instead Marv & Louis ran along the beach and each carried a kelp pod above their head.

"Look at us, Shelly Cat, we have flying fish!" said Marv & Louis.

They all laughed and laughed.

The little Sanderling birds ran to and from the waves so fast that their little legs became a blur.

"Let's go run with the Sanderlings!" said Shelly Cat.

The three friends ran behind the little birds when the wave retreated, but they were not nearly as fast as the Sanderlings and it seemed only seconds before the wave came back.

"Run!" Shelly Cat said, "Run!" Louis grabbed onto Marv's hand. They all barely managed to get away from the wave and stay dry.

"Well," grumbled Marv, "that certainly wasn't my idea of fun".

Shelly Cat said, "It was quite an adventure though wasn't it?"

"Yes," said both Marv & Louis, "but we don't want to do it again!"

"Splash" came the sound as the huge pelicans plunged into the sea catching fish in their pouches for dinner. The mice sat on Shelly Cat's back while she took a cat nap.

"That dive was a 10!" said Louis.

"Yes," said Marv, "that one was spectacular".

The pelicans dived again and again into the water to catch fish. Splash, splash, splash!

"Oooo," said Marv & Louis together.

Shelly Cat By the Sea was glad she wore her special fish necklace today. She closed her eyes and daydreamed that she might have fish for dinner.

Shelly Cat held up a strand of small kelp pods, which she thought looked like an amber necklace in the sunlight. Marv was enjoying looking at small, shiny Olive shells. Louis picked up a sea shell and suddenly squeaked in surprise.

A hermit crab popped out of the shell and said to them, "What are you doing you silly mouse?"

"Sorry sir," Louis said, "I didn't know this was your home."

"Well it is," said the hermit crab, "now put me back in the tide pool please."

Shelly Cat picked up the hermit crab and carefully put him back in the tide pool.

"Well that's just one more reason to leave shells on the beach," said Shelly Cat.

Marv & Louis shook their heads up and down because they were still a bit surprised and couldn't quite manage to talk yet!

"Let's go see the sail boats at the beach today!" said Shelly Cat to the mice.

"OK," said Marv & Louis.

They were all very excited. Louis decided to take a paper flag to wave. Shelly Cat found a small red flag in the back of her closet and carried it to the beach.

"I don't see any sailboats, where are they?" said Marv.

"They're right here," said Shelly Cat as she pointed to the little blue jelly fish called By the Wind Sailors, which were being washed up onto the beach.

Marv threw up his hands into the air and said "I thought we were going to see real sail boats!"

Shelly Cat laughed. They all had a good time watching the jelly fish "sail boats".

Sometimes when Shelly Cat, Marv & Louis walked on the beach, they were sad to see how much trash was left on the beach and then washed up by the ocean.

"Shelly Cat," Louis said, "why do people come to the beach and leave their trash behind?"

"I don't know," said Shelly Cat, "maybe people just don't realize that it will wash into the ocean."

The three friends decided to spend their time at the beach picking up as much trash as they could. Shelly Cat carried a little red sand pail, which she filled up with bottle caps, glow sticks and lost sunglasses. Marv found some plastic straws and picked them up. Louis found a deflated balloon.

"It is hard work," said Shelly Cat, "but if we don't pick up the trash who will?"

Marv said "It would be bad if the fish and turtles ate this stuff."

The three friends were glad that they had spent time helping to clean up the beach.

Every time the three friends walked on the beach, they saw lots of mussel sea shells. Shelly Cat loved to look at the inside of the mussel shells, which shimmered in the sunlight like a tiny rainbow.

Louis said, "Shelly Cat can you please make this mussel shell stand up in the sand for me?"

"Of course, Marv," said Shelly Cat.

After a moment Marv announced, "This is my new beach house".

He stepped inside the hinged shell and used a seaweed branch to sweep the floor of his sea shell house!

Louis said, "My shell is a boat!"

He climbed into his mussel shell and used a bit of seaweed as an oar so he could pretend to paddle his boat to see Marv's new beach house. Shelly Cat smiled at how much fun they always had at the beach.

"Do you want to go watch the Snowy Egrets dance today?" Shelly Cat said to Marv & Louis.

"Yes, let's go watch dancing birds!" they both said.

At the beach, they all sat on beach rocks to get a good view. The Snowy Egrets flew up into the air & spread their wings. The sea breeze ruffled their pretty feathers.

"It's so magical!" Shelly Cat said.

"Yes, it is!" said Marv & Louis.

Shelly Cat By the Sea and the mice walked along the shore at low tide picking up sea shells washed up by the waves. Marv carefully held a small Kelp Scallop sea shell that was very delicate. Louis found a tiny broken bit of a sea urchin shell. Shelly Cat picked up a rusted hotel key that washed up onto the beach with a tag that read "Sea View".

"Leave the shells on the beach," she told the mice, "but I'm going to take the key home with us so a fish doesn't eat it by mistake."

"OK," said the mice as they put the shells back on the beach.

"Didn't we have a fun time today?" said Shelly Cat.

"We did!" said both the mice together.

One day Shelly Cat By the Sea found a long frond of seaweed and held it up.

"It looks like a scarf!" Shelly Cat said.

Even though the seaweed scarf was quite damp, Shelly Cat draped it around her neck and did a little dance while humming.

Marv said, "I just read about seaweeds and that's called a feather boa kelp."

Louis pointed out to Marv some bright yellow-green leafy seaweed growing on a rock.

"Louis, that is called lettuce seaweed and you can eat it", said Marv.

Louis sat right down and munched on the seaweed lettuce.

Marv searched for a while and then ran over to show Shelly Cat and Louis a purplish-red, seaweed blade that was covered with bumps and was dripping wet.

He told Shelly Cat and Louis, "This is called a Turkish towel!"

"That wet seaweed wouldn't dry anything!" said Shelly Cat.

They all laughed until their sides hurt.

"Let's go see the polka-dotted sea gull chicks," said Shelly Cat one sunny morning.

Louis said, "I want to see polka-dotted birds!"

"Let's go!" said the mice together.

Shelly Cat took them to a bluff where they could all see the sea gull chicks. Just to be sure they were safe, the mice hid underneath a Sea Lavender plant.

"They really have polka-dot feathers!" said both the mice with big round eyes.

"Now I've seen everything!" Marv said.

"No you haven't!" Louis said.

"Bark, bark, bark!"

Shelly Cat and the mice were a bit frightened. Dogs could be a bit scary sometimes.

Shelly Cat stopped and peered through the daisies on the bluff.

"Oh," said Shelly Cat, "it's just the sea lions barking out on the reef, come and take a look."

The mice bravely peeked from behind Shelly Cat.

"Oh!" said Marv & Louis, "they sure are loud!"

"Bark, bark, bark!" said the sea lions!

One sunny afternoon Louis ran up carrying a golden Jingle Shell glinting in the sun while he shouted, "Look, I found the sun, I found the sun!"

Shelly Cat laughed and raised her paw up under the golden sun setting on the horizon & said, "No, I found the sun & look I can hold it, too!"

Marv just threw up his arms & rolled his little pink eyes at both of them!

"Its Harbor seal pupping season," said Shelly Cat, "let's go see the baby seals!"

Marv & Louis both jumped up and down with excitement. Shelly Cat put on a sun hat and Louis brought one of his paper umbrellas to shade him from the sun. They all waved hello to the Harbor seals and one adorable spotted harbor seal pup waved back!

"Oh," squeaked Louis, "I just love the seal pups!"

"I do, too!" said Marv.

Shelly Cat was very happy.

Shelly Cat, Marv & Louis walked on the beach early one morning. Marv looked at each sunset clam shell he found to see if they really did all look different just like each sunset. (They did.) Shelly Cat had on a very fancy straw hat with hearts that sort of jingled when she walked. Louis paraded along carrying his paper umbrella. Suddenly a group of dolphins surfed in on a wave very close to the beach! Shelly Cat, Marv & Louis were all very surprised and delighted. They all waved to the dolphins.

"What a great way to start the day," Shelly Cat happily thought to herself.

Indeed it was.

Shelly Cat especially loved this time of the year when the tall red flowers bloomed.

Marv proudly told Shelly Cat, "I looked this plant up in a nature book and these are Aloe Vera plants."

"Thank you, Marv what a nice thing to do," said Shelly Cat.

"Wow, I'm glad I wore my blue hat today!" said Shelly Cat as they all watched how the Cormorant bird's turquoise throats glittered in the sun.

"They have turquoise eyes," said Marv.

Louis said, "Look, there are aqua eggs in their nests!"

Marv waved to a Cormorant who fluttered his wings in a beautiful bird dance.

Shelly Cat said, "How lucky we are to live by the beach!"

Shelly Cat By the Sea loved baskets. She often used baskets to carry sea shells and other important stuff.

"Do you think that we could make our own baskets?" asked Shelly Cat.

"I'm sure we can," said Marv & Louis who had lived in a grass nest when they were born.

They all went to the marsh at the bay. Shelly Cat busily gathered reeds and grasses. She wore a necklace with a tiny glass fishing float just in case she got a bit too close to the water. Marv quickly started to weave a small basket. They were both amazed at Louis who took marsh grasses, split them into small strips and wove a wonderful hat!

"Wow, I never knew that you were such wonderful basket weavers!" said Shelly Cat to Marv & Louis.

"I want some pine nut seeds," said Louis one day.

"Will you come with us to gather them from the pine cones?" Marv asked Shelly Cat.

Of course Shelly Cat agreed because she loved to play with the pine cones while the mice gathered up the pine nuts. Marv brought a little basket he had made to carry the pine nuts in. Shelly Cat wore a necklace with a little red bell, which tinkled musically as she played with a pine cone. Friends doing things together is always fun, even chores!

Shelly Cat said to Marv & Louis, "I bet all the wild sun flowers at the marsh are blooming now from all the winter rain".

"Can we go see?" said Marv & Louis together.

"Yes," said Shelly Cat, "let's go".

The edge of the marsh at the bay was filled with a sea of bright yellow sun flowers

"Oooo," they all said together, "aren't they beautiful?"

"Listen to all the buzzing bees," said Shelly Cat, "they are busy collecting pollen to make honey."

"All the birds are singing, too!" said Marv.

"Buzzing bees and birdsong make me very happy," said Shelly Cat.

Shelly Cat said to Marv & Louis, "Tonight the moon is full and it will be high tide and Grunion Fish will come out of the ocean up onto the beach to lay their eggs."

"It's impossible for fish to come out of the water and do that," said Marv.

"Just wait, you'll see," said Shelly Cat.

When the moon came up and it was dark, they all walked to the beach. Marv & Louis were astonished to see the fish wiggle their way out of the ocean. The fish sparkled in the moon light as they laid their eggs in the sand on the beach. Marv waved hello to the fish as they arrived, but Louis was a bit scared so he stayed behind Shelly Cat and just watched from a safe distance. Shelly Cat carried a colander to catch some of the Grunion fish to look closer at them, but decided not to disturb them. The moon smiled and the stars twinkled. What an adventure they all had by the sea!

The paper parasols were folded up and put away for the night. Marv & Louis were already sleeping soundly in one of Shelly Cat's old hats. I bet they were dreaming about their beach adventures.

"Tomorrows another day," thought Shelly Cat to herself as she sat on her purple silk cushion and purred herself to sleep.

Shelly Cat, Marv & Louis are lucky to be such good friends and have adventures at the beach, aren't they? Yes, they are! Good night! See you in the morning at the beach!

Coastal Wildlife Reference for

"Shelly Cat By the Sea: Adventures at the Beach"

Harbor Seal & Pup

Brown Pelicans

MARINE MAMMALS

California Sea Lion
- *Zalophus californianus*

Common Dolphin
- *Delphinus delphis*

Harbor Seal
- *Phoca vitulina*

SEAWEEDS

Feather Boa
- *egregla menziesil*

Giant Kelp
- *macrocystis spp.*

Sea Lettuce
- *ulva spp.*

Turkish Towel
- *chondracanthus exasperatus*

SEA SHELLS

California Horn Shell
- *cerithidea californica*

Californian Mussel
- *mytilus californianus*

California Sunset Clam
- *gari California*

Eccentric Sand Dollar
- *dendraster excentricus*
- *sea urchin class*

Kelp Weed Scallop
- *leptopectin latrauratus*

Pacific Calico Scallop
- *argopectin cularis*

Purple Dwarf Olive
- *olivella biplicata*

Pearly Jingle Shell
- *Mollusca bivalvia*

Brandt's Cormorant

Sea Lavender

HORE BIRDS

randt's Cormorant
- *phalocrocorax penicillatus*

rown Pelican
- *pelecanus occidentalis*

anderling
- *calidris alba*

nowy Egret
- *egretta thula*

estern Sea Gull
- *larus occidentalis*

THER

y-the-Wind Sailor
- *velella velella*

alifornia Grunion
- *leuresthes tenuis*

ermit Crab
- *pagurus spp.*

acific Mole Crab (sand crab)
- *emerita analoga*

PLANTS

Aloe Vera
- *aloe barbadensis*

Bush Sunflower
- *asteraceae*

California Cordgrass (Salt Marsh Plant)
- *spartina foliosa*

Sea Lavender
- *plumbaginaceae*

Seaside Daisy
- *erigeron glauca*

Torrey Pine Tree
- *pinus torreyana*

Sand Dollars

Made in the USA
San Bernardino, CA
09 March 2018